THE CROCODILE IS COMING!

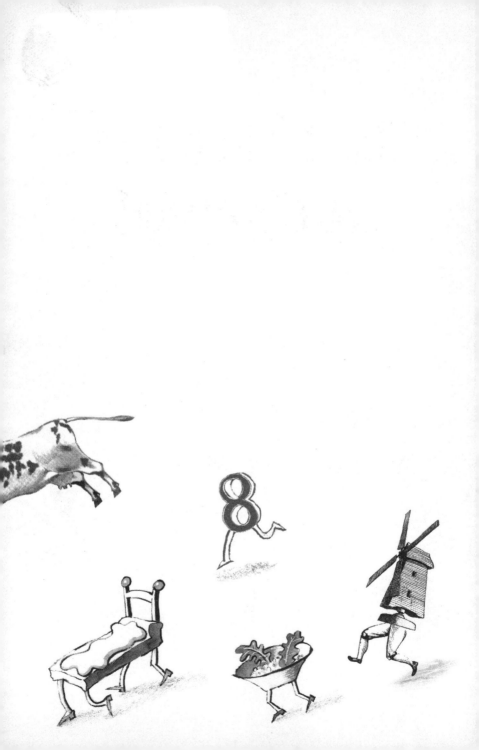

The Crocodile is Coming!

Poems by
June Crebbin

Illustrated by
Mini Grey

WALKER BOOKS
AND SUBSIDIARIES
LONDON · BOSTON · SYDNEY · AUCKLAND

CONTENTS

INTRODUCTION

I like poems that rhyme
And I like poems that don't,
I like poems that puzzle me
And I like poems that won't
Fit easily and have a very long line in the middle;
I like poems that are not too short
And poems that ramble on and on
I like poems that think they are
A song…

I like reading poems – and I like writing poems! When I was writing the poems for this collection, I knew I wanted to use lots of different shapes and sizes. But I had to be patient. First comes the idea, the moment when you know you have a poem beginning. Then I think of the shape the poem is going to be, its pattern. Then, as my idea grows, I decide on its length and whether it needs to rhyme. Sometimes only part of the poem rhymes as in "The Robin" and "My Rabbit" and sometimes there's no rhyme at all as in "Cobweb Morning".

I like to write story poems like "The Dinosaur's Dinner" and poems which have a very long title (see page 8). I like to write acrostics like "Steam Train" where each letter of the title begins a new line. I like writing conversation poems like "Teatime", or poems which count syllables like "The Peacock Pavement".

In every poem I hear the words in my head over and over, long before I put pencil to paper. I hear its rhythm or its repetition. I love to play with words as in "A Hard-to-Crack Case", or use words to make the shape of the poem as in "Kite". I like jokes and twists in the tail and surprises – I even like poems which begin with a question like "Why Don't You...?"

*But I don't like
Poems that end in a question –*

Do you?

I hope you enjoy reading my poems – and writing your own!

June Crebbin

WARNING TO A PERSON SITTING UNDER AN APPLE TREE IN AN AUTUMN GARDEN ON A SUNNY AFTERNOON WITH THEIR NOSE STUCK IN A GOOD BOOK

Directly up above you hanging by a thread
An apple's getting ready to thump you on the head.

FIRST AND LAST

I like to be first in the playground,
I like to stand by the tree,
I like to imagine that all this space
Belongs entirely to me.

I walk from the tree to the waste-bin,
I walk across to the hedge,
I zig-zag across to the bushes
And then I go right round the edge.

When my friends arrive in the playground,
That's when the real games begin.
But I'm not a very fast runner
So I don't often try to join in.

Sometimes they say, "Are you playing?"
As I practise bouncing my ball,
But they always ask too many people.
I'd rather stay by the wall.

And when I hear the whistle
At precisely five to nine,
And everyone rushes and pushes,
I choose to be last in the line.

I like to be last in the playground,
I take a last look around, and then,
I promise myself that tomorrow
I'll be first in the playground again.

KITE

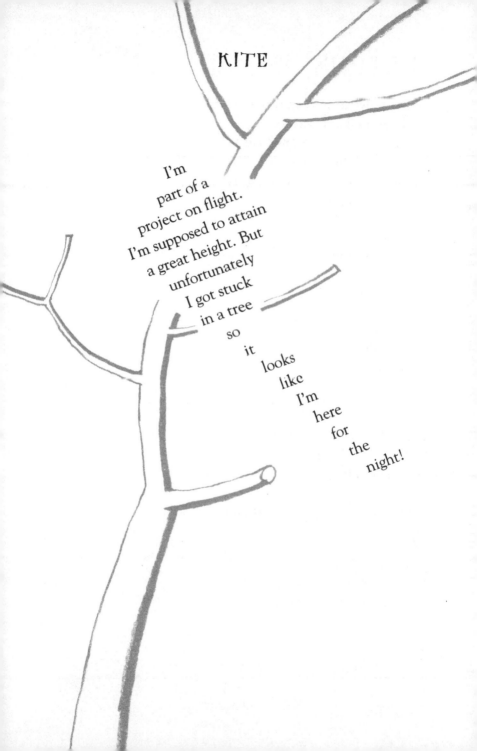

I'm
part of a
project on flight.
I'm supposed to attain
a great height. But
unfortunately
I got stuck
in a tree
so
it
looks
like
I'm
here
for
the
night!

THE ROBIN

I tried to write a poem today,
I tried to make it rhyme,
I tried to get the meaning right
But every single time
I thought I'd got the hang of it,
I thought I'd got it right,
I found I couldn't think of a word
To rhyme with bird
Or, that is, robin.

I didn't want to say
I saw a robin.
It was bobbing
Along and sobbing.
Because it wasn't.

So I started again.

Once, last winter, in the snow,
I was out in the garden
At the bird table,
When I turned round.
And saw, on the path beside me,
A robin.

It was so close
I could have touched it.
It took my breath away.

I have never forgotten
The red of it
And the white snow falling.

ONE OF THOSE DAYS

Kevin's ripped his paper,
Kelly's lost her pen,
And Tim is having trouble
With his nine times ten.

Mary isn't sure
Where her ruler's gone,
And Sally-Ann is certain
All her sums are wrong.

Matthew can't remember
What the teacher said,
His face and page are white
But his eyes are red.

Gemma thinks her writing's
Getting far too small,
If there's any further shrinking
There'll be none at all.

Christopher, by accident,
Bumped into Jane,
And the smudge has spoilt her picture
And she wants to start again –

Oh, the floods are flowing freely,
There's a lot of rain about,
Thank goodness when it's playtime
And the sun comes out!

13

MY RABBIT

When my rabbit
is out in his run,

he digs up the ground
like a dog,

washes himself
like a squirrel,

sits on his back legs
like a kangaroo,

leaps and twirls
like an acrobat,

but

when he eats a cabbage leaf,
as is his daily habit,
he delicately nibbles it
EXACTLY like a rabbit!

WELL, I *NEVER*!

The other day I swallowed a pig,
It was ever so big;
The other day I swallowed a goat,
It slid down my throat;
The other day I swallowed a farm,
I came to no harm;
The other day I swallowed a bull,
I was really full;
The other day I swallowed a horse,
Delicious, of course,
And only last week I swallowed a hen,
I'm not sure when;
The other day I swallowed my pride
And was sorry I lied
About the pig and the goat,
        the farm and the bull,
        the horse and the hen,
So I started again…

The other day I swallowed a tooth –
Now, that's the truth!

GOING ... GOING ... gone

CALLING ALL STARLINGS
CALLING ALL STARLINGS

BREAD FOR THE TAKING
YESTERDAY'S BAKING

FLY DOWN THERE STRAIGHT AWAY
EAT-IN OR TAKE-AWAY

CALLING ALL STARLINGS
CALLING ALL STARLINGS

calling all sparrows
calling all sparrows

peck up a bargain
clean up the garden

crusts only left now
tell all your friends now

calling all sparrows
calling all sparrows

calling a fieldmouse...

16

SPIDER

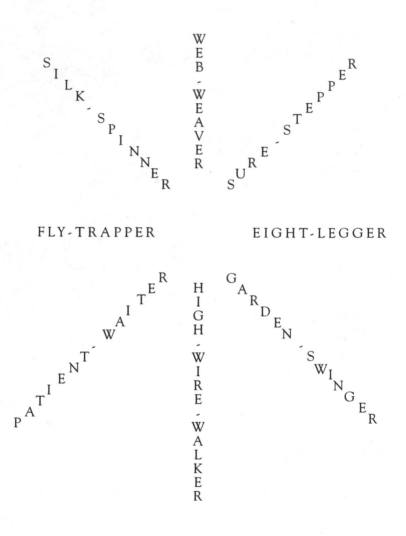

SILK-SPINNER

WEB-WEAVER

SURE-STEPPER

FLY-TRAPPER   EIGHT-LEGGER

PATIENT-WAITER

HIGH-WIRE-WALKER

GARDEN-SWINGER

THE COW WHO LIKED JUMPING

There once was a cow
With great good sense,
Jumped over a gate
And over a fence,

Over a river,
Over a tree,
Over a mountain,
Over a sea,

Over a jungle,
Over a plain,
Over a forest
And back again,

Back to her field
And the same old ways,
Chewing the grass
In a bit of a daze.

So was she content
With the usual scene?
Did she go back
To her normal routine?

NO!

She went for the Big One.
Yes, one afternoon,
Daisy the Cow
Jumped over the moon!

IN THIS TREE

In this tree
are greenflies, sawflies
and beetles burrowing;

In this tree
are ferns and mosses
and a thread of honeysuckle;

In this tree
are butterflies
feeding on sunlit leaves,

woodpeckers
searching for insects,

squirrels nesting;

BULL
IN
FIELD

20

In this tree
are acorns
and a notice saying:
BULL IN FIELD.

What's that noise?
What's that thundering noise
behind me?

Help!

In this tree
are all these things

and me.

GREAT-GRANDFATHER'S WATCH

This was great-grandfather's watch.
It has a gold face, a gold strap,
a second hand,

a place that tells you the date,
and dashes for numbers,
but I know what they are.

Great-Grandpa was ninety-seven,
the oldest person in our family,
the oldest person anyone in my class knew.

He used to sit in a chair,
and shake my hand with his good one,
and say, "Hello young man."

He used to sing "Gorgonzola Cheese"
and wear a Panama hat indoors
and give me chocolates.

He won't be there now
when I visit my Leicester Auntie.
I won't see him ever again.

But this was his watch.
He gave it to me,
and it's still ticking.

TWINS

we are .... we are

very like .... very like

each other .... each other

except .... except

for one thing .... for one thing

I'm your sister! .... I'm your brother!

KISSES

My little sister gives me
a doggy kiss,
LICK! LICK!
with her tongue.

My little sister gives me
a butterfly kiss,
FLICKER! FLICKER!
her eye lashes on my cheek.

My little sister gives me
an Aunty Chrissie kiss,
SLOBBER! SLOBBER!
drippy as a dishcloth.

But she can't give me
a sandpaper kiss
like my cat.

Only Jemima
can do that.

TEATIME

What's for tea today?

    What do you fancy?

Oh, bed and butter,
Ham and leg,
Knees on toast
And trampled egg,
Chocolate lake
And leaf stew,
Smashed potato:
That'll do!

    Fancy!

Or oodles and oodles
Of plop suey and poodles...

    Well, it's fish and chips.
    How's that for starters?

Great! What's for afters?

    Apple pie and mustard!

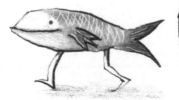

THIS IS THE DAY

This is the sort of day
I should like to wrap
In shiny silver paper
And only open when it's raining;

This is the sort of day
I should like to hide
In a secret drawer to which
Only I have the key;

This is the sort of day
I should like to hang
At the back of the wardrobe
To keep me warm when winter comes;

This is the day
I should like to last for ever;

This is my birthday.

I LIKE POEMS...

I like poems that rhyme
And I like poems that don't,
I like poems that puzzle me
And I like poems that won't
Fit easily and have a very long line in the middle;
I like poems that are not too short
And poems that ramble on and on,
I like poems that think they are
A song.

But,
I don't like
Poems which end in a question –

Do you?

NEWSƒLASH

There has been a disaster
At the Magic Show.

Rosalie was cut in half
And looks likely to remain so.

We understand that the magician responsible
Is not available for comment
As he seems to have vanished
Along with his doves, magic wand
And sixteen coloured handkerchiefs.

A white rabbit, however,
Is being held for questioning.

Rosalie is said to be
Putting a brave face on it
Which is not easy
When she hasn't a leg to stand on.

If anyone can supply
Human superglue
Invisible sticky tape
Or the whereabouts of the missing magician,
The police, not to mention Rosalie,
Will be delighted to hear from them.

BEWARE!

The crocodile is coming!
It's heading for the pool,
It's swaying down the road
From the local Primary School.

Better keep your distance,
Better close your doors –
Beware the fearful clamour
From its ever-open jaws!

Be careful not to stumble
As you hurry from the street:
Remember that the crocodile
Has sixty tramping feet!

Through the city jungle
The creature marches on.
Wisely, shoppers stand aside

And wait until he's gone.
It's going to cross the busy street –
It starts to leave the path –
Attacked by snarling traffic
It's completely cut in half –
The head continues on its way,
The tail, delayed, just laughs
And runs to catch it up
At the Municipal Baths.
The crocodile is swimming
In the Public Swimming Pool,
But soon it will be heading
For the local Primary School.
So, better keep your distance,
Better if you try
To find a place to hide
While the crocodile goes by!

ON A MONDAY MORNING

A sing-along song

What shall we do with a naughty schoolboy?
What shall we do with a naughty schoolboy?
What shall we do with a naughty schoolboy
On a Monday morning?

Throw him in the bin with the mouldy rubbish,
Throw him in the bin with the mouldy rubbish,
Throw him in the bin with the mouldy rubbish
On a Monday morning.

Oh dear, the smell's disgusting!
Oh dear, the smell's disgusting!
Oh dear, the smell's disgusting
On a Monday morning!

What shall we do with a naughty schoolgirl?
What shall we do with a naughty schoolgirl?
What shall we do with a naughty schoolgirl
On a Monday morning?

Hang her from the ceiling and tickle her tootsies,
Hang her from the ceiling and tickle her tootsies,
Hang her from the ceiling and tickle her tootsies
On a Monday morning.

Oh dear, the smell's disgusting!
Oh dear, the smell's disgusting!
Oh dear, the smell's disgusting
On a Monday morning!

What shall we do with an angry teacher?
What shall we do with an angry teacher?
What shall we do with an angry teacher
On a Monday morning?

Lock her in the cupboard with a hungry tiger,
Lock her in the cupboard with a hungry tiger,
Lock her in the cupboard with a hungry tiger
On a Monday morning.

Oh dear, the smell's disgusting!
Open up the door, the smell's disgusting!
Here comes the tiger – and the tiger's smiling!
On a Monday morning.

NON-SWIMMER

I can't swim.
No one knows
At this school yet.
I'm not letting on
To anyone.
I'll just forget my kit.

I've done it before.

When the teacher says:
"Who is a swimmer?"
I keep still.
And when he says:
"Who is a non-swimmer?"
I keep very still.
And no one notices.

I've done it before.

When I get home
My mother says:
"When's your swimming day, then?"
And I say: "Thursday."
I don't mean to.
I just forget.

One thing's for sure.
Mum'll remember my swimming kit.

She's done it before.

If ONLY

I'm waiting to see the headmaster
And my legs are beginning to ache.
I've been standing here ever since lunch time,
How long is he going to take?

He said, "Wait there till I'm ready,"
And his meaning was perfectly clear,
I've been standing here over an hour.
He could have forgotten I'm here.

I wish I'd never played football.
I wish I wasn't at school.
"Rules are made to be kept," he says,
And I do. Well, I do, as a rule.

But today, I just couldn't help it
And I would have scored a goal,
Only the ball went too high and it vanished,
So I went through the hedge, through the hole.

I knew by the crash where I'd find it.
I knew by the pieces of glass.
It looked like the whole of the greenhouse
Was scattered about on the grass.

I offered to pay for the damage,
I offered to sweep up the mess,
But the lady who lived there ignored me
And asked for my name and address.

She wouldn't listen to reason,
She wouldn't listen at all.
She telephoned the headmaster
And confiscated my ball.

I'd rather be doing my lessons
Than standing here on my own.
I know he's still in there, because
I heard him answer the 'phone.

I wish I could turn back the clock,
I wish I could go back in time.
People keep passing and staring
As though I'd committed a crime.

I didn't do it on purpose.
If only he'd let me explain,
I'd give him my Scout's word of honour
That I'd try not to do it again.

They'll be painting by now in the classroom.
He's wasted my whole afternoon.
I wish it was over and done with –
Surely he'll talk to me soon.

THE LOLLY'S LAST REQUEST

I'm an ice-cold lolly

With a joke upon my stick

I'm a getting-warmer lolly

With a disappearing trick

I'd rather drip inside you

Than be a drip beside you

So please lick me quickly

Quickly lick me

Quickly quickly

Lick me

Lick me

Lic

L

L

L

L

L

!

A HARD-TO-CRACK CASE

If suits go in a suit-case,
Pencils in a pencil-case,
Books go in a book-case,
Do police go in a police case?

If tea goes in a tea-bag,
Shopping in a shopping-bag,
Pegs go in a peg-bag,
Does a school go in a school-bag?

If a horse goes in a horse-box,
Money in a money-box,
Toys go in a toy-box,
Are there windows in a window-box?

If eggs go in an egg-cup,
Coffee in a coffee-cup,
Fruit goes in a fruit-cup,
Is there butter in a buttercup?

If flowers go in a flower-pot,
Honey in a honey-pot,
Stew goes in a stew-pot,
Does fuss go in a fuss-pot?

All these questions needing answers
Make a hard-to-crack case.
The only answer I can find is
I'm a little nut-case!

IN THE PARK

slide

the

of

top

the

to

up

way

long

a

It's

b
u
t
f
u
n
w
h

i
z
z
i
n
g
d
o
w
n
o
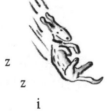
ntheotherside.

41

CLASS 2 AT THE DINOSAUR EXHIBITION

Ann admired the brontosaurus,

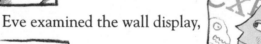

Ben began his lunch,

Carol couldn't find her pencil,

Daniel drew a stegosaurus,

Eve examined the wall display,

Frances found a fossil footprint,

Guy got lost and began to cry,

Helen hurried to help him,

Ian imagined meeting a mammoth,

John joined in,

Katie kept on asking questions,

Lee left his bag on the bus,

Mitesh missed the mammoth's tusk,

Nigel noticed it at once,

Oliver ought never to have touched it,

Peter put it back,

Queenie queued in the shop for ages,

43

 Richard reached the end of his worksheet,

Stephanie stood in the dinosaur's footprint,

 Thomas took her picture,

Ursula used up all her paper,

 Vikram vanished,

William wandered off to find him,

 Xanthe explored the way to the exit,

Yasmin yawned and then

 Zoë zipped up her anorak and said:
"When are we coming again?"

44

NOTHING

What   did

to it!   you

Nothing   say,

Miss.   Kevin?

easy   Nothing

It's   Miss.

nothing.   Oh

can say   really?

you   That's

how   clever.

know   to   like   I'd

GIANT MOTH

One windy day,
when I was taking a message
across to the Infant School
with my friend,

I saw
a giant moth
land
on the school field.

It was so big
I could see clearly
its yellow and brown markings.

As it rested
I saw
each wing lift
and tremble
before it rose in the air again.

My friend said
it was only a big leaf,

But I said,
I think I know a Giant Moth
when I see one.

COBWEB MORNING

On a Monday morning
We do spellings and Maths.
And silent reading.

But on the Monday
After the frost
We went straight outside.

Cobwebs hung in the cold air,
Everywhere.
All around the playground,
They clothed the trees,
Dressed every bush
In veils of fine white lace.

Each web,
A wheel of patient spinning.
Each spider,
Hidden,
Waiting.

Inside,
We worked all morning
To capture the outside.

Now
In our patterns and poems
We remember
The cobweb morning.

UPS AND DOWNS

Teachers like you
to
sit up
shut up
and put your hand up
when you have something to say.

Teachers like you
to
calm down
sit down
and put your pencil down
when you've only just picked it up.

Teachers like you
to
speak up
make your mind up
and stand up straight
when they're talking to you.

Teachers like you
to
settle down
put your ruler down
and keep your voice down
when it's supposed to be choosing time.

Teachers,
like you,
have good days
and bad days!

JOINED WRITING

I am learning to do
Joined Writing.

I have written pages
of sand and land and band.
I have written thousands
of book, look, took and cook.

I can now write
enormous, multiplication and kangaroo
without taking my pencil off the paper…

By now most people have been given a pen.

I have thirty-three ticks,
seventeen "Good Efforts",
one "Good"
and a "What happened to you today?"

When I get "Excellent",
I will get a pen.

RACE AGAINST TIME

And here we are now,
Ready for the start,
Pencils poised,
Breathing heavily,
Eyes on the starter…

And they're off!
Four fives, two fives, three fives,
Eight fives –
Eight fives? Eight fives?
FORTY!
And they're
Over that one
And on to the next –
And coming up now
To the half-minute mark.
Half a minute,
Half a minute to go
And one of them is trailing –

No, no,
He's still there,
He's still in the race –
Nine fives, nine fives?
Nine fives?
FORTY-FIVE!
And into the straight,
Down the paper,
And they're
Coming up to the finish
With five seconds to go,
Four, three, two –
And they've finished!
With a second to spare
And they're
Breathing freely now.
Papers over,
Pencils down.

THE DINOSAUR'S DINNER

Once a mighty dinosaur
Came to dine with me,
He gobbled up the curtains
And swallowed our settee.

He didn't seem to fancy
Onion soup with crusty bread,
He much preferred the flavour
Of our furniture instead.

He ate up all our dining-chairs
And carpets from the floor,
He polished off the table, then
He looked around for more.

The television disappeared
In one almighty gulp,
Wardrobes, beds and bathroom
He crunched into a pulp.

He really loved the greenhouse,
He liked the garden shed,
He started on the chimney-pots
But then my mother said:

"Your friends are always welcome
To drop in for a bite,
But really this one seems to have
A giant appetite.

You'd better take him somewhere else.
I'm sure I don't know where,
I only know this friend of yours
Needs more than we can spare!"

And suddenly I realized
I knew the very place,
And when I showed him where it was
You should have seen his face –

I don't think I've seen anyone
Enjoy a dinner more,
I watched him wander on his way,
A happy dinosaur!

The council did rebuild our school,
But that of course took time…
And all because a dinosaur
Came home with me to dine!

CHARLIE

In the meadow near our school
A giant carthorse stands,
We feed him crusts and apple cores
From flattened, outstretched hands.

I used to snatch my hand away
From Charlie's lowered head,
I worried that he'd miss my gift
And eat my hand instead.

But now I know his gentleness,
The way he clears my hand,
His muzzle soft as summer grass
Blowing in the wind.

MAKING THE COUNTRYSIDE

Take a roll of green,
Spread it under a blue or blue-grey sky,
Hollow out a valley, mould hills.

Let a river run through the valley,
Let fish swim in it, let dippers
Slide along its surface.

Sprinkle cows in the water meadows,
Cover steep banks with trees,
Let foxes sleep beneath and owls above.

Now, let the seasons turn,
Let everything follow its course.
Let it be.

I SAW A DUCKLING

I saw a duckling puffing by
I saw a steam train in the sky
I saw a rainbow eating grass
I saw a cow as smooth as glass
I saw a pond turning round
I saw a windmill leap and bound
I saw a cricket plough a furrow
I saw a tractor dig a burrow
I saw a rabbit in a coat and hat
I saw a farmer with his cat
I saw all these when I went for a ride
Out and about in the countryside.

RIVER

boat-carrier

bank-lapper

home-provider

tree-reflector

leaf-catcher

field-wanderer

stone-smoother

fast-mover

gentle-stroller

sun-sparkler

sea-seeker

THE STREAM-DIPPING PARTY

I went to a stream-dipping party,
With my wellies, a net and a jar,
We waded into the water,
We were told not to go in too far.

Johnny and Ben caught some tiddlers,
And Amy fished out a ball,
Even Dan caught a leaf and a button,
But I caught nothing at all.

So I waded just a bit further,
I could see a shiny bright tin,
I was stretching my net out to grab it,
When I tripped on a stone – and fell in.

I went to a stream-dipping party,
With my wellies, a jar and a net,
Everyone there got something,
But only I got – wet!

STEAM TRAIN

Smoke pours from the engine as the steam
Train prepares to leave, clouding itself and
Everyone watching before settling into its journey
Along the valley, close to the river,
Mountains rising in the distance.

Tickety-tack, tickety-tack, picking up speed, it
Races past sheep and cows, bridges, trees,
Aiming for the sea, straight as a rocket, or looping
Into bends, hugging the curve, slowing for the viaduct –
Now, along the straight, smoke flows like a banner.

GOODNIGHT

"Goodnight," said the frog, "I am burrowing deep
Into the mud for my winter sleep."

"Goodnight," said the hedgehog, "I'm off to my nest,
It's time I went for a good long rest."

"Goodnight," said the bat, "my feet are strong,
I'll hang in a cave the winter long."

"Goodnight," said the dormouse, "I shall be
Curled in my nest at the foot of the tree."

"Goodnight," said the toad, "I've found a deep hole
To keep me warm from the winter's cold."

"When you wake in the spring," said the kindly sun,
"I'll be here with my warmth for everyone."

THE JUNGLE SALE

Once, before I went to school,
When I was only four,
I went to the village Jungle Sale
With Mary from next door.

The hall was full of people,
But, as far as I could see,
No sign of a lion or tiger,
Not a single chimpanzee.

And where were the man-eating spiders?
Gorillas? Cockatoos?
Mary said that she'd buy me
A present – but what could I choose?

There were piles of clothes on the tables
That stood around the hall,
But no sign at all of an elephant
On the white elephant stall.

Still, I did go home with a monkey
With wrap-around arms and tail,
And whatever Mum says, I've kept him –
He's definitely Not for Sale.

BRIC A BRAC

HOME-MADE CAKES

JUNGLE SALE
ENTRY
50p

GIANT

There's a giant in our classroom,
He comes from far away,
We've made him warm and comfortable,
We're hoping that he'll stay.

He wears a suit of armour
To shield him from attack,
It's hard to tell which part of him
Is front and which is back.

He keeps himself inside himself
Until he moves about
When eyes and head and everything
Gently ripple out.

His giant foot begins to spread,
His giant eyes explore,
And when he's eaten all there is
He looks around for more.

He waves his giant feelers,
He leaves a giant trail,
I never tire of watching
Our Giant African Snail!

WHY DON'T YOU...?

Why don't you join the choir?

Well, you have to sing on your own, don't you?

Don't be silly.
A choir means everyone singing together –
A chorus of voices.
Sometimes we sing hymns or carols,
Sometimes we sing songs – with ACTIONS!
We're in all the school concerts,
We sing to old people,
We take part in competitions,
We go all over – even to the cathedral.
We have a really good time.
You'd enjoy it.

OK. How do I join?

First, you have to sing on your own –

PLEAS~E!

Bumble bee, bumble bee,
Fly away home,
Leave my naked toes
Alone!

Bumble bee, bumble bee,
Don't you know
Another place where
You can go?

Bumble bee, bumble bee,
When I doze off,
I don't need you, so
Buzz off!

CITY RIVER

wall-slapper

factory-passer

rubbish-receiver

backstreet-winder

bridge-nudger

steps-licker

park-wanderer

summer-shiner

ducks-supporter

choppy-water

crowd-delighter

onward-traveller

THE BOAT BUS

The bus sails through the rain:
From the top deck, I can see
The greedy river flowing
Where green fields used to be.

Rain batters the windows,
Streams across the glass,
Trees, with a stutter of gun-fire,
Attack us, as we pass.

We sway from village to village,
Up many a hill and down,
Trying to keep a look-out
For the lights of the distant town.

The bus stops in the High Street:
We step on to land again,
Where pavements shine in the street light
And only puddles remain.

DOWN OUR STREET

Down our street lives a strange old man,
Heats his bed with a warming-pan,

Eats ice-cream in the middle of the night,
Reads in bed by candle-light,

Paddles in the gutter when the rain comes down,
Never, never, never goes shopping in town,

Goes out fishing if it's wet or fine,
Hangs his wellies on the washing-line,

Sleeps outside when the weather's warm,
Rides his bike in a thunderstorm,

The happiest man you'll ever meet
Is my friend Ben from down our street.

THE PEACOCK PAVEMENT

Down
These steps,
Beneath the
Floor of this old
Shop, lies another
Floor, a Roman pavement,
Fashioned out of tiny stones
Set in swirls and coils and petals,
And at its centre, a peacock, proud,
Spreading his tail of blue glass feathers.

THE MEETING OF THE WAYS

The Motorway said, "I'm the best by far,
I am built for the high speed car."

The High Street said, "No, I'm the tops,
In me you'll find all the well-known shops."

"Trees line me," said the Avenue,
"I'm the obvious choice of the well-to-do."

Said the quiet Close, "They choose me too.
I'm sure I'm nearly as good as you."

The Crescent cried, "I go right round the bend.
You'll never find me with a blocked-off end!"

The Cul-de-Sac at once replied,
"But I am calm and dignified."

"Which way is best is hard to agree,"
Said the mighty Drive. "But I'm sure it's me."

Under the blue and cloudless sky
The footpath quietly passed them by.
It made its way to the top of the hill:
And across the fields it is travelling still.

FINDING A FRIEND

"Will you be my friend?"
said the rubbish to the river.
  "No, never."

"Will you be my friend?"
said the spider to the fly.
  "Not I."

"Will you be my friend?"
said the lion to the deer.
  "No fear."

"Will you be my friend?"
said the boat to the sea.
  "Maybe."

"Will you be my friend?"
said the child to the summer days.
  "Always."

TO THE BEACH

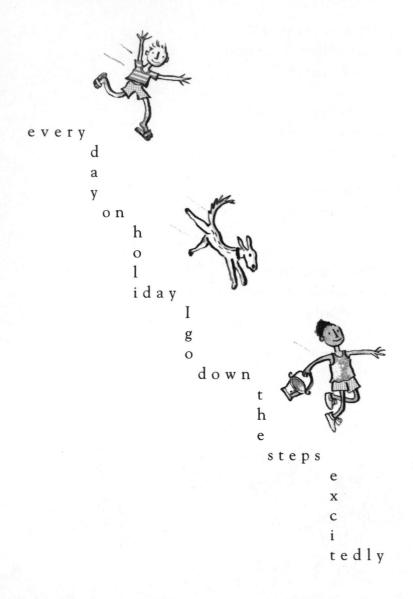

every
   d
   a
   y
     on
         h
         o
         l
          iday
               I
               g
               o
                  down
                        t
                        h
                        e
                           steps
                               e
                               x
                               c
                               i
                              tedly

to jump the waves and swim in the sea

MY GRANNIES

I hate it, in the holiday,
When Grandma brings her pets to stay –
Her goat, her pig, her seven rats
Scare our dog and chase our cats.
Her budgies bite, her parrots shout –
And guess who has to clean them out?

My other Gran, the one I like,
Always brings her motorbike,
And when she takes me for a ride
To picnic in the countryside,
We zoom up hills and whizz round
bends –
I hate it when her visit ends!

HOLIDAY MEMORIES

When I was on holiday
I went to Timbuktu,
I wrestled with a jaguar
And boxed a kangaroo.

I journeyed into jungles,
I swam the deepest sea,
I climbed the highest mountain
And a monkey-puzzle tree.

I chatted to a seagull,
I met a big baboon,
I floated on a moonbeam
Until I reached the moon.

I visited the planets,
I lit up all the stars,
I gossiped to a parrot
Travelling to Mars.

I sailed across the ocean,
I drove a Greyhound bus,
I rode across the desert
On a hippopotamus.

I heard a mermaid singing,
I fought a killer shark,
I grappled with a Grizzly
In a wild Safari Park.

I chased a band of pirates
Completely round the bend.
And now the summer's over
And so is this – THE END

for Caroline Royds & Ben Norland

First published 2005 by Walker Books Ltd, 87 Vauxhall Walk, London SE11 5HJ

2 4 6 8 10 9 7 5 3 1

© 2005 June Crebbin   Illustrations © 2005 Mini Grey

The right of June Crebbin and Mini Grey to be identified as author and illustrator
respectively of this work has been asserted by them in accordance with the Copyright,
Designs and Patents Act 1988

This book has been typeset in Goudy

Printed and bound in Great Britain by Creative Print and Design (Wales), Ebbw Vale

British Library Cataloguing in Publication Data:
a catalogue record for this book is available from the British Library

ISBN 1-84428-965-6

www.walkerbooks.co.uk